I'd like to be a

Cowboy Poet

*and other Country Poems
by a Country Boy*

*Bill May
Kearney, NE*

Copyright © 1996

ISBN: 1-57502-391-1

Printed in the USA by

*M*ORRIS
PUBLISHING

3212 E. Hwy 30
Kearney, NE 68847
800-650-7888

Author Bill May

$\mathcal{S}$pecial recognition to
Nancy Christensen for many hours of typesetting.
To Judy Rozema and Letitia May for proofreading
and a big thank-you to Jodene Cloudt
for all the artwork and illustration in this book.

Thank-you ladies. Without your help, this book
would not have been possible.

Bill

Mildred and Ross May

I dedicate this book to Mother and Dad.
Who, like many others, endured the hardships
of the depression years and farming
during the "Dirty Thirties".

Contents

The Sows Are In The Yard

I came in from farmin'
one day at noon
to feast upon a meal.
There my wife was cookin'
in all of her appeal.

She didn't say anything
as I washed my hands and face.
I was just about ready to sit down
and say our table grace.

I said, "What's the matter dear?"
and then I noticed the muscles in her jaw
were awfully hard.
And through clenched teeth she blurted out
"Your sows are in the yard!"

I grabbed my cap and headed out,
and to the garden went
· and there they were,
ten big sows going up and down each row.
Kinda like cultivators--
maybe more like plows
doing their thing to help our garden grow.

1

The Red Hamp sow was eating cabbage--
no cole slaw for us this year.
and the York destroyed the potatoes
and then grinned from ear to ear.

The boar chomped on carrots.
The black sow got out in haste.
She had tried to eat an onion
and didn't like the taste.

The little runty one wasn't good enough
to sell as a pig, so I kept her for a sow.
She had a touch of bull-nose
that left her with a crooked snout.
She must have thought she'd died
and gone to heaven
the way she was eating Brussels sprouts.

The four red Duroc sows
(they're my kind of hogs)
they were doing me a favor
so for a little while I let them be.
They were rootin' up the cauliflower
and killin' the broccoli.

Where was the red spotted sow.
She wasn't to be found
and there I saw her back in Mom's flower bed
sniffin' like a hound.

I ran like heck to get her out of there.
For she had gladiola bulbs a-flyin' through the air!
Well, I finally got them out
and back into their pen.

2

And then I found the problem.
The electric fence was shorted out, again.

I got it workin' and back to the house I went.
We ate that meal in silence
as if it was during Lent.

The next day was sale day
at our local auction barn.
And I had one thing I had to do--
that was to haul them from the farm.

Now when you're a small hog farmer,
you are really out of business
when you sell your breeding stock.
But if you're a married hog farmer,
you better consider your wife's feelings quite a lot.

Well, I kicked the tires on the trailer
and hooked it to the truck.
I got those hogs all loaded
and off to town I struck!

I thought that I could be back before she missed me,
but you guessed it--no such luck!
When I got back she met me at the driveway
and said, "Where have you been?"

I replied those sows won't bother you any more
for I just hauled them in!
She said it wasn't really necessary
to sell off all my hogs.
Just keep the fencer workin'
and the dang sows in their pen.

Well, what's done is done!
I parked the trailer and started back to work
and then I remembered the hog check
in the pocket of my shirt.

3

So I took it to the house
and she was getting ready
to go shopping one more time,
which I didn't think was really necessary.

But again she was cheerful
about to do her thing.
She asked "Is there anything you need?
or what can I do for you?"

I said, "Well, if you have time,
you could put this hog check in the bank."
"Gladly", she said, "for my account is almost dry."
She needed some hog money to help her to "get by".

She said she'd even get some cash.
Tonight she wanted us to go out and have a little bash.
Well, once more this hog farmer had "been had".

But when I did my evening chores
I didn't have the heart
to tell her I kept back
ten replacement gilts
and I could surely find a boar.

Now being a married hog farmer
is kinda like going off to school.
Each day you can learn a lesson--
some easy---some kinda cruel.

The easy ones we tend to forget
but the ones that really go down hard
will stick with us forever,
like the day the sows got in the yard!

Halloween

Halloween like Christmas
comes but once a year.
For Halloween, we think of masquerade
and costume parties;
for Christmas, peace and joy and cheer.

Now when it comes to costume parties
I'll admit I am a little bit gun shy
and by the time this poem is finished
you'll understand the reason why.

It was way back in the forties
and I was a kid in school.
We had this all school party
and it left me feeling like a fool.

This party was at our teacher's house
she invited all the kids.
We were to all dress up in costume
and keep our identity hid.

She said there'd be this contest
and there would be a prize
for the one who for the longest time
could fool the other guys.

Well, I wanted to win that contest
but that posed a bigger problem for me.
Whatever should I dress up like,
whatever could I be.

Should I be a pirate or a cowboy
or Disney's Goofy dog with outlandish paws
or a farmer or a fat man
or dress up like Santa Claus.

My sister heard of my predicament
and said, "Let me give your costume design a whirl"
and came up with the big idea
to dress me like a girl.

She covered my head and face with a stocking
and said, "That should do the trick."
My facial features were distorted
but my lips I could not lick.

She put on me a blouse and skirt
and high-heeled shoes as well.
She said the other kids wouldn't know me,
there was no way to tell.

On my head she put a hat.
Around my neck some simulated pearls.
She said, "They will never guess you're a guy,
you look like another clumsy girl."

With confidence I went to that party.
But there was one thing we overlooked, I guess.
They couldn't tell who I was but
the girls recognized my sister's dress.

So there I was, sentenced for the evening.
I wouldn't win the prize.
A guy dressed like a girl
but they had blown my disguise.

This was a long time ago
and of my age I do not brag,
but back there in the forties
we didn't hear of guys dressing up in drag.

We had a treasure hunt
and were to go to neighboring houses if we dared
and get a list of things
the teacher had prepared.

Can you imagine this farm kid
dressed like a girl
running down the street.

All was going really quite well
until my long underwear
came down around my feet.

It was of ultimate humility
that I had a taste.
Sprawled on the ground
with my underwear around my ankles
and my skirt around my waist.

It didn't take long to get myself righted
and things put back in place
but how could I go back to that party?
How could I save my face?

We played other games and had refreshments,
drank some root beer covered with foam.
And was I ever relieved when it was over
and time to go back home.

Today if I get invited to a costume party
now that I'm a man,
I just say I have a previous commitment,
I have other plans.

So young boys if you go to a Halloween party,
reconsider your costume.
Think about it more than twice
and if you will allow me, I'll offer this advice.

Dress like Mickey Mouse, Smoky Bear
or that little flying squirrel
but never, never, never, never
let them dress you like a girl.

Windmills

What happened to our windmills?
You won't see any on your way to town.
I guess it was our windstorms
and the tornadoes blew them down.

They never will be rebuilt;
there is no need of course,
now we use electricity
to power our water source.

Some people have ornamental windmills
standing on their lawns.
I guess it reminds them of a different era
and days that are long gone.

You see decorator windmills
made of plastic, brass or tin.
I saw one made from old used barbed wire,
but its wheel it did not spin.

Leila has a decorator windmill
hanging on the wall.
It's made from wooden clothespins--
they too aren't used anymore at all.

I guess it reminds her of days long past,
and as the story goes,
the windmill pumped the wash water,
and the clothespins dried the clothes.

She washes in an automatic washer
and after it has spun,
she puts them in the dryer
and plays with her grandsons.

Jacob will smile at you with his mouth
and Jarrod can smile at you with his eyes.
They are two of the cutest little country guys.

With their burr haircuts
and little overalls,
they would make a good calendar picture
to hang upon the wall.

She has to answer lots of questions
but to a grandma this is fun.
This is quality time--not wasted time,
and the laundry still gets done!

Getting Old

I don't mean to push you aside
or put you on a shelf
but as I write this poem
it will be a poem about myself.

My hair is getting thin on top,
the sides are getting white,
but it's just because I used too much Brylcream
when I was young and chasing girls at night.

If you see me with my neighbor,
don't think it's so very strange
if I just introduce him as my neighbor
'cause sometimes I can't remember his name!

When I look at things up real close
or even far away,
my eyes will kinda fill with tears,
I know it can't be my glasses
because I've had them over a dozen years.

Through the years I've lost some teeth
or you might say they just went south.
But if I was a black-faced sheep or white-faced cow,
you'd call me broken mouth.

My kids accuse me of getting senile
or maybe a little weird.
The guys at work all tell me I'm getting so dang ugly
I should hide behind a beard.

My face is getting rough and wrinkled.
It's just from the summer's hot sun
and the winter's bitter cold.
I'm sure that's the only reason,
'cause I sure ain't getting old!

My neck is a little stiff,
my head won't turn very far each way
kinda like a toad.
Now I have to turn clear around
just to see whose pickup it was
that just went down the road.

My hands and arms and elbows and my shoulders too,
seem to be stiffening up because they don't
do the work they used to do,
like pounding nails, sawing boards,
and shop work like we did in school,
'cause now for even the smallest jobs,
I use power tools.

My chest has slid down a bit,
my belly is now a paunch.
I tell my wife it's kinda wrong when she makes
statements like,
I look like I could be about seven months along.
I tell her to be patient and maybe it will go away,
just like hers always did when she looked that-a-way!

I used to be in the hog business
and a fun job was sortin' hogs
because when I had to round them up
I could run just like a dog.

When pigs got out and chasing them
and putting them back in
wasn't near the job that it is now
'cause I haven't got the wind.

I've always tried to take care of myself.
I've never drank a beer or got hooked on nicotine,
but I'm sure my lungs suffer from one awful thing I did.
You see, I smoked a home-made corncob pipe
when I was just a kid.

I'd hollow out a broken corncob
and we had lots of them.
Then I'd take a piece of copper gas line,
blow out the dirt and that would make the stem.

I'd have a pocket full of matches
and then I'd get some sour dock weed seed.
I'd sit on a bucket in the corn crib
and with my smokin' I'd proceed.

I'd get my pipe all lit up
and some expertise I did acquire.
And all the time I was smokin'
it was just like eatin' fire!

I did this when Dad was out a workin' in the field
and Mom had gone to town
and it's only by the grace of God
I didn't burn the corn crib down!

My knees won't bend as sharp as they once did
and my legs stage their own protest, of course.
And now I find it is much easier if
I'm standing on a bale of hay
when I get on a saddle horse!

My toes are bent and crooked.
They go this way and that
and I have figured out the reason
and of the cause I am very sure.
You see, when I was little,
I went barefooted and I stepped in cow manure.

You say that wouldn't cause it
but here is the most convincing clue.
When my feet got fertilized,
my toes outgrew my shoes!

In spite of all my infirmities
I am really quite healthy
and I sleep just like a log.
But my wife says that with all the noise I make
when I am sleeping, it's more like a boar hog.

She says my snoring keeps her awake all night,
but it ceases each morning a little after five.
I tell her that's my built in indicator
to let her know I'm still alive!

I'm kinda like a traveling salesman's late model car
that you might see a "for sale" sticker on--
It's not the years that hurt me,
it's just the miles I've gone!

State Fair

My neighbors think I'm goofy
for this hobby that I have.
They say it's foolish to be raising Belgian horses
when I could be raising exotic calves.

They are entitled to their opinion
but their feelings I do not share.
I'm not in it for the money,
but rather the camaraderie with other Belgian breeders
at our once-a-year State Fair.

So in this little poem,
I'll try to let you know
something about what it's like
to be in a Belgian Draft Horse Show.

You pull your trailer up to the Draft Horse Barn.
Your friends greet you one and all
as you unload your horses
and begin to decorate your stalls.

You wait your turn at the wash rack,
and then you scrub them down.
This will be the cleanest they have been
since the last time they came to town.

You get them all sudsed up
with Brilliance show shampoo.
I guess I used a handful,
where a little dab would do.

I wash the mane; I wash the tail,
and all four legs get soaked up with that shampoo.
It not only makes them squeaky clean,
it makes them smell good too.

I rinse them once; I rinse them twice;
surely that will do.
And then I notice that in the crease along the back,
there is still a trace of that shampoo.

I squirt them off one more time
this will have to do.
My friends are beginning to scowl at me.
They want to wash their horses too.

Now I lead them up and down the street
to help to get them dried.
I begin to hear remarks
that they look like Budweiser horses.
They think that they are Clydes!

I get asked all kinds of questions,
questions of every sort.
Like, "How much they eat?",
"How big they are?" and "Why are their tails so short?"

Some little boy wants to ride my horses,
but before he whines and begs,
I say I must get back to the stalls
and put sulfur on their legs.

Next, I take some auto body putty
or Quick Poly would also do.
I proceed to build and shape the hooves
to be as big as those scotch bottom shoes.

I fill the splits and holes and cracks;
on the outside hinds I build a flare.
I want everybody thinking
that we have tremendous feet
under that Belgian mare.

I cover my handiwork with hoof black.
They look quite nicely I must say.
They look just like the real thing
if you're standing far enough away.

Now it's the day for judging,
the morning of the show.
Joe Allen is up at 4:00 o'clock,
already on the go.

He's busy cleaning stalls and brushing horses
and filling up some water pails.
Phil Callahan is up on the bench braiding manes,
and if they can get Dave woke up,
he'll be busy tying tails.

The Eberspacher crew is busy doing everything;
getting their show string ready
to enter that show ring.

It all looks so in order
even the alley way is swept.
I ask them where Darrel is;
they say he must have overslept!

Starting with the stallions,
each class must wait its turn
to go in the ring before the judge,
for the placing it will earn.

My mare is relaxed and patient and resting one hind leg,
her head is hanging halfway down,
eyes half closed and her lower lip begins to droop.
My colors are slightly tarnished,
invariably when I tie a tail,
I drop the ribbons in the poop.

At last our time has come.
The PA system blares:
"Exhibitors, please get ready,
and bring in the older Belgian mares."

We leave the barn and head for the coliseum show ring
down the street.
It stirs the very soul of a horseman
to hear the cadence of those big shod hooves
striking on concrete.

We enter the ring at the trot
and line up along the rail.
Then each in turn will be called out before the judge
to be inspected from the head back to the tail.

We're asked to walk and trot our horses
to show how well they go.
This is just a part of showing horses
at any draft horse show.

He checks the head, the ear, the eye
to make sure everything is right.
He quickly slips two fingers in the mouth
to check for overbite.

He goes down the line to compare the front ends,
there is no indication of his preference yet.
And then the judge goes around behind
to see how well the hocks are set.

We wait with anticipation
as the judge begins to make his picks,
to see who will be pulled out
to be in the top placing six.

First out is an Eberspacher Belgian
with a Ludwig mare close behind.
And then another Eberspacher mare
gets taken from the line.

Right now I begin to thinking
it certainly would not hurt
if next year when I show horses,
I'd wear an Eberspacher shirt!

Rangely Farm, Umberger and Sunnybank
make up the final three.
By gosh, the six places are already filled
and the judge did not pick me.

He lines them up in single file,
head next to tail
and then quickly glances back
at those of us left along the rail.

He may switch a horse or two in line,
but this class is almost done.
Like I said before,
I'm not in this for the money,
I do it just for fun.

We congratulate all the winners
and tell each exhibitor we're glad that they are there
and we'll look forward to seeing them all
at next year's big State Fair.

Now lately, I've been thinking of branching out
in this game of livestock exhibition
and to understand my reasoning
should not be so very hard.
It will be kinda like playing bingo
with several bingo cards.

I think I'll go to showing fancy chickens.
It should be a whole lot easier than showing horses
ever will be you know.
I won't need a gooseneck trailer
or a dually pickup to get my chickens to a show.
I'll just take the family car
and to a chicken show I'll go.

I think a small bowling bag
will hold all my chicken showing junk.
I'll throw that in the back seat of my wife's LaSabre
and I'll haul the chickens in the trunk.

And when I reach the fairgrounds
and find my chicken's designated cage
where he'll take up residence
and feel like he has center stage.

I'll give him a cup of water
and half a pint of feed.
That should be all that any show chicken
would ever need.

I won't need a white show bridle
to hold my chicken on the rail.
Chickens don't have manes to roll
and you don't tie show chickens tails.

I won't need a farrier
or any showing stocks.
And I've never heard it reported
that feeding too much corn
will "blow" a chicken's hocks.

20

I won't need scotch bottom shoes
to make his right foot turn a little bit to the south.
Chickens don't have teeth to float;
they're all a little bit parrot mouthed.

Then when the horse show gets finished
I'll saunter over to the chicken barn
to see how well my chicken did.
If he should have been named Grand Champion,
I'll be just as tickled as a little 4-H kid.

But if he does not do so well,
I can still leave the fairgrounds
feeling somewhat dignified.
For if my chicken does not win his class,
I'll eat that sucker fried!

I'd Like To Be A Cowboy Poet

I'd like to be a cowboy poet
and write cowboy poetry
But can I really be a cowboy poet,
if I'm not a cowboy first, you see?

Oh, I have some of the credentials
that good cowboys have,
I have a little place that's mostly hay and grass
and some cows that are going to calve.

I wear cowboy clothes
like shirts that snap,
high-heeled boots and
good old Wrangler jeans
and I eat everyday cowboy grub
like 'taters, beef and beans.

But I don't ride the range like cowboys do,
if my cows I want to see,
since I feed my cows with a pitchfork,
when I call them, they will come to me.

When they're all lined up and eating hay,
that's when I get the counting done,
It doesn't take long to make the head count,
when you only count to twenty-one.

I have bursitis in my roping shoulder;
I can't raise my right arm.
So when my cows see me with a lariat,
they know there is less than one chance in a million
that I will cause them any harm.

I can't write poems about snow capped mountains
because mountains I do not see.
If I want to see mountains,
I have to look at the National Geographic Magazine
or some travelogue on TV.

I can't write poems about the desert sagebrush
mesquite or even prickly pear,
because I've been all over my pasture
and they're not growing there.

I write poems about corn and hogs and cows
and grass and the blessings of God sending timely rains
because that is what we see and hear
and need the most here on the Central Plains.

I always wanted to be a rodeo cowboy,
I thought riding saddle broncs would be for me,
but all I ever did was go to the Burwell Rodeo
and sit in the bleachers, Seat 27, Row 22, up in Section C.

You're probably wondering with my small place
and so few cows,
how do I manage to survive.
I'll admit I have a side line,
it's a rendering truck I drive.

It makes me feel kinda like a cowboy
as I do this job for which I have been hired.
I go all over the country and gather cows
for someone else after they've expired.

I've pulled cows from mirey, swampy, sloughs,
some cowboys call them bogs.
I've pulled cows from river banks,
if I could get my truck close enough among the fallen logs.

I've pulled cows from wrecked semi-trailer trucks.
I've pulled cows from rough hill pastures
when they've been lightning struck.

I've pulled cows from cornfields
when they've eaten more than is good for them.
I've pulled cows from slaughter house pens
when the inspector says, "Condemned".

I've pulled cows from highway right of ways;
they usually don't go very far,
if they've been in a high speed collision
with someone's family car.

I've pulled cows from veterinary clinics
if they don't survive the surgery.
The vet had done all he could,
and then ended up calling me.

Like a cowboy I enjoy a good clean practical joke,
especially if I can pull one
on the modern-day college folks.

Every now and then a college kid will tell me
I must have the worst of jobs any man has ever had.
I say, "Oh, if you get paid $45,000 a year
for driving that truck, then dead cows don't smell so bad."

At this his mouth drops clear open,
his eyes will open wide.
He exclaims, "My goodness sakes alive.
For that amount of money,
that truck I too could drive."

I shake my head and tell him,
"There is a whole long waiting list.
The positions are all filled,
There is no need for you to apply."

And then I chuckle as I drive away,
leaving him standing there
just wishing he was the other guy.

If you think I should have a label
for writing this kind of poetry,
then maybe just a dead cow---boy poet
is what you should call me.

Little Meg Elizabeth

It was last June.
In fact, it was exactly Father's Day
that your Mama and your Daddy told us the news
that you were on the way.

We had to wait all summer
and then all through the fall.
We would have to wait halfway through the winter
for you to appear at all.

The doctor said February 14th was your E.T.A.
I thought what perfect timing
for a brand new little sweetheart
to come along our way.

Then it was January 30th
still the first month of the year,
Your mother called me that evening
and said you were already here.

Ten little tiny fingers. Ten little tiny toes.
Two little dark shining eyes and a little button of a nose.
Only 19 inches long, from your little head down to your feet.
A perfect little person and you are all complete.

I look forward to the future
and all the fun that we can have.
When you can go with me in the pickup
to look for baby calves.

No doubt you will want to run in the grass
with your little feet so bare.
I'll warn you to be careful
for there are hidden cactus there.

26

I'll show you how to catch a grasshopper,
and hold him, and watch him spit tobacco juice.
I'll show you how he can unhook one jumping leg
and still jump away when we turn him loose.

I'll show you the beauty of the sunset
and then before it gets too dark,
I'll help you look in the clumps of grass
for the nest of a mother meadowlark.

And as we look at the tiny eggs,
if you notice one is different from all the rest,
I'll explain to you it was probably a mother cowbird
that also found the nest.

I'll help you pick wild flowers
when God sends rain upon our land,
and I'll show you how it tickles
when you hold a fish worm in your hand.

I'll try to teach you to enjoy God's creation
and all there is to see.
And I'll show you how good ripe mulberries taste
when you eat them off the tree.

And if we should get purple stains
on your little dress,
I'll be the one that will confess
so they won't put the blame on you,
but lay it all on me.

Your Mama and your Daddy and your Grandma
have lots of love for you,
But always remember little Darlin'
Your Grandpa loves you too!

My Bullride

I always wanted to be a rodeo cowboy
I thought, what a perfect way
to earn a living making 8-second rides
and collecting the winner's pay.

Last night I got my chance
I was wearing my loud-colored cowboy shirt
and Wrangler jeans, the official cowboy pants.

We were at this bull riding contest
and they had an extra bull
an old Brahma, big and stout.
They offered to let someone make an exhibition ride
and not just turn him out.

I climbed up on the chute gate
and eased down on his back.
They put the bull rope on him
and started pulling up the slack.

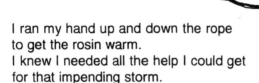

I ran my hand up and down the rope
to get the rosin warm.
I knew I needed all the help I could get
for that impending storm.

I slipped my hand into the loop
and put the suicide wrap around my wrist,
tucked the end of the rope under my little finger
and pounded it down tight with my other fist.

He stood there just like a gentleman
slowly twitching his ears.
No doubt he was tallying up all the cowboys
he'd bucked down through the years.

I had my spurs jabbed in,
and my toes turned out
I was ready to see what
bull riding was all about.

I screwed my hat down tight
until it was just above my eyes.
and what was going to happen to me next
I did not realize.

I nodded for the chute gate
and they swung it open wide
it was then I felt things come alive
in that old Brahma's hide.

I might have stayed with him a half a jump
and then like a bomb that bull exploded.
He was no longer between my knees.
I know that I was looking down
but I was seeing the top side of the trees.

I hit the ground like a bag of salt.
I felt just like a toad
when he gets run over by an 18 wheeler
when he tries to hop across the road.

My lights went out and all was dark and still
except for the sound of birds
a twittering in my head.
I thought I had bucked over the great divide
and I surely must be dead.

As I lay there in the stillness,
my mother's voice came through so clear and full.
"I told you that would happen
if you tried to ride a bull."

If only I had listened
and heeded her advice,
my head wouldn't feel like it was filled
with half-cooked Minute rice.

Then someone from the E.M. squad said,
"Stand back a little and poke him with a stick.
Sometimes when a bull rider comes back to life
he'll give a violent kick."

I knew that he was safe enough
no harm would come to him.
I wasn't about to kick anyone
with both my legs wrapped around my chin.

Then someone must have struck a match.
I saw this tiny flame.
I knew if I ever walked again,
the guys would call me lame.

Then that tiny flame grew brighter
and once again I could begin to see.
I realized I was leaning back in my recliner chair
and the bull was on TV!

Driving Cats

I had lots of big ideas
when I was a little kid.
I bet my folks kept wondering what would be
the next idea to pop into my head.

I was just a little fellow,
maybe only five,
I had this big idea that I was a teamster
and that I could break some cats to drive.

I'd go out and catch some cats
and bring them in the house.
Then I'd take a ball of cord string,
make cord string harness, cord string bridles
and put cord string bits into their mouth.

When I had them all harnessed,
I'd take them back outside.
I'd put them down as a team
and then I'd proceed to drive.

I'd tell them to "Get-up"
but they wouldn't even go.
Then I'd have to use my foot
and boot 'em with my toe.

Then they would run off
and get tangled in some weeds.
I'd have to go cut up my harness
and do it with some speed,
before they choked down and gagged
and finally run out of air.
There were times I'd get so mad
I didn't really care.

I thought it should be simple
for them to learn to drive,
but it must have been impossible
for that goal ever to arrive.

I kept on planning in my head
how it would be so fine
to have a tiny wagon pulled by two smart-stepping cats
and me holding cord string lines.

I didn't give up easily.
I kept trying to train those cats.
But it wasn't in their heads to drive.
They would rather catch some rats.

We've all heard the old-time saying
"If at first you don't succeed, try, try again."
I don't really know who said it
or where he came up with that.
But I know he was a man
who never tried to hitch and drive a cat.

The Old Farmhouse

The other day I drove into an old farmyard
while doing what I do,
and immediately I was impressed
by the panoramic view.

The house was situated on a little knoll
where it was standing still,
and one could look across the valley
to the far off distant hills.

There were telltale signs that the barn
had at one time been painted red,
along with the corn crib, chicken house
and the now empty, long hog shed.

Those buildings when new and painted red
must have made just quite a sight,
wearing their new coats of paint
and the house all painted white.

These buildings served their purpose well
to keep both man and beast from harm
and I'm sure that once upon a time
this was a model livestock farm.

I believe the old house contained a story
and just what would the story be,
if that old house could come alive
and it could talk to me.

It could tell me who the builder was
and how he worked so hard
to build up all the buildings
that made up this good farmyard.

It would tell me how it made his wife so happy
and how proud he must have been
when the last of the paint went on
and the last shingle nail driven in.

It could tell me when they lived there in the good years
and the ones that were so dry
and it could also tell each year it was,
when it heard a newborn baby cry.

It could tell me just how many boys and girls
lived within its walls,
where it saw so many skinned knees and elbows
from a hundred childhood falls.

There would be so many memories
of things that happened long ago,
of children playing in the yard
in summer and in winter in the snow.

The large front porch must have been
a favorite place to play
and it was a place of comfort
when things did not quite go their way.

It was a place to nurse hurt feelings
until their tears had dried,
and someone crawled under that porch
to retrieve the remains when the mother cat had died.

It was a place to relax in comfort
for the Mother and the Dad
where they could talk things over
and let settle the big supper that they had.

Each evening after supper
the kids would climb the stairs
and just before they jumped into bed
they were taught to kneel and say their prayers.

It could tell me just what year it was
when the rooms were lit with rural electricity,
and how the children's faces beamed that first Christmas
they had a lighted Christmas tree.

There would be countless stories about the kids
growing up the way that farm kids do
and that is just what this house would tell us,
if it could talk to you.

There would be all kinds of memories
of the kids going off to school,
and each evening they came home
and did their chores because that was the rule.

The oldest son, he loved the farm
and he grew up so very fast,
he had a dream that he would be a partner with his dad
but this dream it did not last.

It must have been late summer
or was it early fall,
that he got a letter saying that he should
answer our country's call.

He was drafted in the army
and this had not been his plan,
but he was sent off to Germany
and he was now a man.

The old house could tell us how it watched the Dad
all broken hearted as he received the news
that his son had stepped on a mine
and died in World War II.

The upstairs bedroom could go on to tell
how from that very room,
each girl had waited with anticipation
for the arrival of her groom.

And how each one was so radiantly
beautiful on her wedding day,
and how the old man's heart ached
each time he gave a girl away.

It could tell me of the hurt it saw
in the old man's eyes,
when one day the youngest son said,
"Dad, I love you, but this farmin' I despise."

"I'm tired of hauling out manure
and hauling in the hay,
I think I'll go live in town,
there's got to be an easier way.

I've had my fill of pulling cockleburs
and piling up the bales,
I think I'll be a salesman
and live off the revenue of my sales.

I'm tired of taking care of newborn calves
in all kinds of ungodly nighttime hours
only to watch them die two weeks later
when they come down with the scours."

So once again it was the Mother and the Dad
living all alone,
in that old farmhouse
on its foundation made of stone.

They lived on for several years
and then on the very anniversary of their wedding day
the old man's wife of forty-seven years
just suddenly passed away.

All alone, the old man lived in the farmhouse,
but it did not much comfort give
and in a few short weeks
the old man just lost his will to live.

Now the house stands there empty
and the upstairs bedroom where someone
used to lay their head
is no longer a restful place for man,
but a pigeon roost instead.

So there it is, an empty farm stead
where life and love and laughter once prevailed
stands there as a grim reminder that all our government's
"Save the family farm programs" so miserably have failed.

But I believe there is a larger lesson
here with deeper meaning too,
It proves that what is written in the Bible
is so very, very true.

How all our earthly treasures
will succumb to rust and rot and decay
and how just through time alone,
they all will fade away.

There is evidence that the moths were there
and that they ate their fill,
first they ate the window sash
and then the window sill.

The thieves broke in and they did take everything of value,
whatever they could find,
and as I looked through the broken window,
there was nothing left behind.

But this old man, all through his life,
he was nobody's fool.
He read and believed the Bible
as if it was an operator's manual for some fine
expensive tool.

He had treasures laid up in heaven
which is not so hard to understand,
for he had trusted Jesus
and he was a Godly man.

What a friend he had in Jesus
who led him by the hand
through Death's long darkened valley,
to the eternal Promised Land.

If that old house could tell me where the cemetery is,
I know that I could find his grave
even though it may be overgrown with weeds.
I would search until I found a marker
on which this epitaph I'd read:

Here lies a farmer,
his body lies resting here below,
but his soul lives on in heaven,
he lived and farmed for God, you know.

Weeds

I hate weeds, but you can't tell it
by looking at my farm.
I have weeds in every field
and some right here by the barn.

There are weeds out in the windbreak,
some weeds in the lawn.
There are weeds in every roadside ditch,
I could go on and on.

Weeds will grow in the softest ground
or in the hardest track.
Weeds will even grow in a concrete sidewalk crack.
Weeds just seem to come from nowhere.

Why, you can have the cleanest summer fallow field,
all worked down, clean and black,
but get just a quarter inch of rain
and the weeds come bouncing back.

Where do all these weeds come from?
You could ask the oldest man in town
and he would simply say
they have always been around.

Now let's go back to the Bible story of Creation.
The best place to start I guess
would be in the beginning
in the book of Genesis.

It tells of God creating man
and giving him a wife,
and planting for them a garden.
They had a leisurely life.

This Garden must have been a small farm
for in it, you see,
was room to grow
just about every kind of tree.

Now Adam and Eve really had it made.
All they had to do was care for the farm
and lounge around naked in the shade.

Now this was a weed-free farm!
What a pleasure that must have been.
There were no nettles to sting their hide
or sandburrs to step in.

And they could eat from any tree
when they were in the mood,
except the "Tree of Knowledge",
it was not meant to be their food.

Then one day they were tempted
and tasted of that tree.
Suddenly their eyes were opened.
They realized they were naked as could be.

41

In the evening they heard God coming
and they were so afraid.
They tried to cover up with leaves
and hide back in the shade.

God was so disappointed
they had fallen into sin.
He said, "I will drive you from my garden
and will never let you back in.

Furthermore, I will curse the ground
and it will bring forth every kind of weed.
From this day on you will have to work and toil
and labor for everything you need."

So from then on man had a job,
not "part-time" but very "full".
Every kind of weed to fight
and cockleburs to pull.

All down through the ages
man has tried to rack his brain
to come up with inventions
to fight weeds after every rain.

We've tried all types of tillage,
to plow and cultivate
and every kind of weeder--
weeds to eliminate.

I thought our work was over
and weed free we would be
when they came out with a chemical
they simply called it 2-4-D.

It was supposed to kill all kinds of broadleaf weeds--
and they would be no more.
But it seems that each succeeding year
there were just as many as before.

Today we have all kinds of chemicals
to fight this war on weeds.
There is Sencor, Banvel, Classic and Resolve,
Beacon, Contour, Buctril and Dual II.
They all have the same purpose,
to eliminate your weeds for you.

But now the men in science tell us
these chemicals are leaching in the ground,
and soon there will be
no clean drinking water left around.

And that these chemicals
will destroy our quality of life.
And they are especially dangerous
for a farmer's pregnant wife.

Wouldn't it be ironic if this chemical warfare
that we've developed to leave our weeds all dead
would somehow backfire on us
and wipe out the human race instead.

What will we do, how can we cope,
and win this age-old fight?
It can be very puzzling,
I sometimes lay awake at night.

Maybe we should back up in time
and fight this fight by hand.
It would make us all a little closer
and keep us on the land.

It would take a lot more farmers,
but then more neighbors we'd acquire.
And if we had more neighbors,
there would be more neighbor kids to hire,
to walk our beans and clean our corn
and fight these pesky weeds.

And I know from experience
when our teenagers go out at night to play,
they will come home much earlier
if they have been pulling cockleburs all day.

There is one more advantage
and I want you to think on it for a spell.
I've never seen a corn knife yet
that would contaminate a well!

See, when God makes a promise
whether it's to Adam and Eve or you and I,
He'll keep that promise
just as sure as the rainbow in the sky.

So let's face it,
my scientific farming friends,
we'll have weeds to fight
until the very day we die!

The Rendering Truck

A few years back when I was farming
I got a little down on my luck.
I needed some more income
so now I drive a rendering truck.

I know you'll wrinkle up your nose
and think this is really gore,
but listen to this little poem
and I will tell you more.

We go to farms and feed lots
and dead animals we remove.
This is a service we provide,
we don't charge you for this service;
we do it for the hide.

Most of you will ask what do we do
with all the animals that we get.
It is most interesting that you can take
something as worthless as a dead animal
and make something out of it.

Of course the hides all go for leather,
which shouldn't bring you any tears
because man has been doing that
for years and years and years.

The fresh lean red beef goes to race tracks
to feed the finest racing hounds.
The #2 meat goes to dog farms
to keep their puppies tummies round.

The #3 meat goes to canneries
to make all kinds of canned pet food.
So don't you eat any of it
regardless of your mood.

All the rest is ground and cooked
for hours with high heat.
You see there are a lot of government regulations
that we're required to meet.

The moisture's removed, the grease expelled
and the dry product is D.R.T. - Dry Rendered Tankage.
Beef by Products, Meat & Bone meal, meat scraps
are other names.

It doesn't matter what you call it,
it all just means the same.

The grease is called feeding fat
and goes to feed lots to put energy in big steers.
Some grease goes to make bar soap
to wash your face and neck and ears.

The finest grade called #1 Bleachable white tallow
goes into ladies' cosmetics.
I think you begin to get the picture now.
Guys, if you've kissed your wife a-wearing make-up,
you've really kissed a cow.

People have all sorts of notions
about this work where I'm employed.
And when it comes to rendering trucks,
people are really paranoid.

They wonder just how I can stand
to drive that smelly truck.
But let me set you straight my friend.
My truck will never smell any worse
than that animal you expect me to pick up.

You have to use a little common sense--
When the wind is from the north,
you don't stand on the south
and if the smell is really bad,
you breathe in through your mouth.

Let me tell you some advantages
of doing what I do.
I get to drive all over the countryside
and see the country view.

I get to see geese and ducks, deer
and wild turkeys
when the river road I drive,
and I really like to see the sand hill cranes
when they at last arrive.

Look at all the signs of spring--
the trees are budding.
The pasture grass is getting green,
watch the baby calves run and buck and play,
and the way the alfalfa is growing,
there may be a pretty fair crop of hay.

It was March 15th this year
when I saw the first gopher run across the road
and I know spring will really be here
when I see or hear a toad.

I see the farmers in the field
late at night and early in the morn.
It's amazing what corn farmers do
just to grow $2.00 corn.

I guess the biggest advantage
and I hope you don't think it's so very cruel
I get to see all the countryside
and my boss gets to buy all the fuel!

Now some people don't appreciate
this free service we provide.
They think we should pay them money
for their dead cow
if we are going to sell the meat and hide.

Now can you think of another nasty job
that someone would come out and do
and when the job is over
they end up paying you?

How about the man who pumps out your septic tank.
Would you expect him to pay
for that awful, stinking, smelly load
that he just hauled away?

Heck, no, you'll pay him about anything
to do a job you wouldn't do.
And you'll even say "Please" and Thank you"
to get him to work for you.

I don't claim to be a philosopher
but I do have a philosophy--
always look on the bright side of things
and you will brighter be.

I try to keep a sense of humor
as I do this job so many people dread--
I'm kinda like a buzzard,
I just go in circles and look for something dead.

Think of me as a cow mortician--
that's really what I do.
But aren't you glad I'm just getting your cow
instead of getting you?

I'm a veterinarian's assistant.
I don't help them with their work--
for that I don't have what it takes,
I just follow them around the country
and take care of their mistakes.

I'm on call pretty much round the clock.
This job isn't from 9 to 5.
So I could haul your dead cow about anytime;
but when I haul mine,
I want them to be alive.

It doesn't matter what the season
or what phase is the moon.
The very best time not to call
is Saturday afternoon!

Now when your livestock becomes dead stock
I know just how you feel.
See, I've been in your shoes
and know your loss is very real.

I know how it is when fat hogs
die from summer's heat.
I know how it is when a young stock cow dies
because she can't get back on her feet.

Or when that baby calf
you've waited 9 long months to get
and now you find him lying there--
lifeless, limp and wet.

And I fully understand when my truck
leaves your yard today,
it's a deep down gut ache feeling
when your horse gets hauled away.

Every now and then
I'm called on to put an old pony down
and I know just what the lady means
when she asks "Could I please get there
before the school bus comes from town."

I still think of myself as a kid
and for the future plan
but lately some of my customers
refer to me as that older gray haired man.

So when you see me in my truck
just think of me as one--
who does an unpleasant job
but a job that must be done.

So go ahead enjoy your life
and do what you like to do
and make use of all that education you have had.

But, please don't look down your nose at me my friend
for if there were no dead stock drivers,
the whole world would smell bad!

Mom And Dad

You deserve some special recognition
in a very special way.
On this Golden Anniversary
of your wedding day.

Fifty years seems like a very long time to us,
but to you they may have gone by very fast.
No doubt when you got married,
there were those who said it wouldn't last.

How could a marriage last
for very many years
when two kids get married
and they are still wet behind the ears?

You were very special partners
on this path you trod.
But you had another partner,
this partner is our God.

You have been such a perfect example
as you lived your life
of what God intended
for a husband and a wife.

When God created man
he said he needs a help-mate,
a partner by his side.
So God performed some surgery
and made the perfect bride.

I believe there is a reason
for this special marriage you have had.
And Mom, I think God made you
especially for Dad.

I have always marveled
at the way you worked together,
quite often hand in hand,
as you did the farming duties
and were stewards of the land.

Whether it be irrigating
or feeding, tending or shearing sheep
or out cutting musk thistles
so a clean pasture you could keep.

Dad, was it by fate or happen-stance
or plain old simple luck
that when you drove the combine
you had Mom to drive the truck.

And when you drove the race car,
for Mom, being a spectator was not enough.
Once again she was your partner
and drove in the Powder Puff.

I remember you working on that car
and then we'd take it for a ride.
You were strapped in the driver's seat
and I'd hang on to the roll bars
as around the corners we would slide.

For many years you were kept busy
keeping your kids in line.
But now that they are grown and gone,
to others you give your time.

Dad, as you drive the school bus,
the kids love you and call you their Grandpa
and they all flock around you
like a year-round Santa Claus.

We're proud of you when you go
on mission trips to other states,
or across the ocean's foam
or conducting Bible studies at
the Harvard Nursing Home.

You are so busy in your lives
but yet you find each day
time to read the Bible
and some time to pray.

You seem so in tune with life,
so happy and always radiating smiles,
and your home is always open
if someone needs a place to stay for a little while.

You always found time to help other kids with little league
or us with 4-H calves.
You were the best adopted parents
an adopted kid could ever have.

You gave us so many memories
of the good times that we had
so from all the kids we say,
"Thank you and congratulations, Mom and Dad!"

Will The Ostrich Replace The Cow?

A couple of years ago, while driving my truck
and going from farm to farm,
I noticed these weird looking buildings,
not very long or wide, but yet they really were quite tall.
Each one had a horse-sized door
but hardly big enough for a stall.

One day I stopped and asked a man what that building
could be used for and its purpose on his farm.
He stuck out his chest and proudly said
"That's my brand new ostrich barn!"

Now he had been to an ostrich promoter's meeting
and he was convinced in his mind
that the ostrich was a good alternative livestock,
the best he'd ever find.

He said the ostrich is the coming thing,
and that I should get in the business
because big money they would bring.

He said one should get in on the ground floor,
the time to start is now.
And in just a few short years,
you'll see the ostrich replace the cow!

55

Now the cow may not be a noble beast,
but she has helped me get to where I am today.
She has caused me to spend my winters
feeding bales and my summers mowing hay!

I herded cows when I was just a kid,
and I milked her in my high school years.
I sold her in the sale barn
when I was a livestock auctioneer.

I drink her milk, I eat her steak
and I sell her calves to pay off the mortgage on our place.
And now I haul her in the cow hearse
when death leaves its grin upon her face.

You see, I've been in some sort of the cow business
just nearly all my life.
And if I were to desert her now,
I'd feel as guilty as if I were cheating on my wife!

So let's analyze this ostrich business
and see if we can determine how
our lives and lifestyle might change
if the ostrich would replace the cow.

Think of all our feed lots,
how dull and uninteresting they would seem,
if they were filled with something
that lacked the cattle color scheme.

There would be no Hereford color
or the Angus blackest black.
There would be no gold of the Gelbvieh.
All this color we would lack.

There would be no red of the Limousin
or white of the Charolais
or any of the black baldys
that are so prevalent today.

Why looking at such a feed lot
would be no fun at all.
We'd miss all the color variation
that comes with crossbred Simmentals.

Yes, an ostrich filled feed lot
would look mighty plain,
for even if you had ten thousand head,
they'd all look pretty much the same.

But there would be some advantages.
You'd have no calving problems.
You could throw away your pulling chains
and for scrap iron your calf puller you could sell,
for if an ostrich does have birthing problems,
you simply take a hammer and break away the shell.

And in the springtime when the frost goes out,
your worries would be lessened
and you could much sounder sleep
because you would know that your ostrich
could still make it to the fence line feed bunk,
even if the Nebraska feed lot mud was four feet deep.

Now if you were going to cook and eat an ostrich,
your problems wouldn't be over yet.
You'd need to read a rule book on
ostrich eating etiquette.

For instance, if you like to eat a drumstick
and on that big drumstick you would chew,
you'd need to call two neighbors in
just to hold it up for you.

Or could you lift it with a chain hoist
and hang it from a tree.
Or would it be fit and proper
just to lean it up against a wall
and hold it steady between your knees?

Or maybe you like to eat the wishbone
and then a big wish you would make.
You'd need a tractor and a pickup truck
if that big wishbone you would break.

Think of all the giblet gravy there'd be,
at least four bushels and a peck
if you diced up that big bird's gizzard
and threw in his big long neck.

They claim that ostrich meat tastes just like beef.
So what really is the purpose anyhow?
If we're going to produce meat that tastes like beef,
why not do it with a cow?

Nebraska would become the ostrich state,
IBP would become IOP,
and McDonald's would have to start their burger count
all over if we eliminate the beef.

We would have to rebuild all our highway overpasses
or maybe not have them at all,
for possum belly, ostrich hauling semi-rigs
would be nearly twenty-seven' tall.

If you think our national debt is high,
consider the mind-boggling expense
if we tried to convert all our range land to ostrich pens,
and enclose them with a seven foot chain link fence.

Think of our western movies.
How different they would be.
They would advertise ostrich boys
and Indians on the overhead marquee.

What would happen to our dairy farmers
that live on dairy farms,
if we were to replace the cow.
It would deal them great economic harm.

They would be reduced to raising silkworms
with those worms producing silk.
Because there is no place to put a milker
on an ostrich or even ostrich milk.

Maybe we could adapt to all the changes
I have mentioned up to now,
but how could we ever have a rodeo
if we didn't have the cow?

I suppose team ropers could head and heel an ostrich,
and calf ropers roping ostriches should somewhat faster be.
For they would only have two legs to tie,
instead of the usual three.

And for our steer wrestlers,
I suppose we could fit dummy horns on an ostrich,
but in order for them to catch that high-headed ostrich pup,
our steer wrestlers would have to learn
to ride their quarter horses standing up.

Then if they made a legal catch and a legal stop
and as they brought that head around,
they would have to twist that neck for twenty minutes
just to get him on the ground.

Then the last event of every rodeo
would seem might tame
because bull riders riding ostriches
just wouldn't be the same.

Think of the bull fighters,
how their self esteem would be beaten down
if they had to admit to all their colleagues
that they were now ostrich fighting clowns.

And the little guy that works in the barrel
whatever would he do.
For if a mean old ostrich stuck his head in the barrel,
he could poke it clear on through.

So there you have my arguments.
I hope you will agree
that we never should allow
something like the silly ostrich
to replace our sacred cow.

Now if you would like to invite us over for an evening
and I hope someday you will,
we could make up some ground meat burgers
and cook them on the grill.

I'd be willing to light the charcoal
and watch the burgers while they cook.
If you would make up some potato salad
open the Old Home buns
and place on each one a lettuce leaf.
You can eat ostrich if you want to,
but please, let me eat BEEF!

Grandma

Grandma Barkdoll was a terror;
this may be hard for you to see.
Just ask my brothers and my sisters.
I know they will agree with me.

Grandma lived near Chicago
and we lived far away.
We lived way out in Nebraska.
We were farm kids,
and we knew about making hay.

Grandma was unhappy about us living so far away
and about this she would make a fuss.
But I always thought it was another blessing
that God bestowed on us.

Every now and then, we'd get a letter
saying Grandma was coming for a visit
and with us she would stay.
I guess all us kids would cringe
and we kinda hated to see that day.

Then mom would give us a lecture
about how we should act and treat her with respect.
She'd tell us to be grateful she was coming,
and greet her with a kiss;
but Grandma had a funny smell so I resisted this.

Now Grandma had an outlook
and she had one goal in mind:
to teach her grandkids how to work
and make them toe the line!

Grandma thought we were most wasteful,
if everything we didn't save.
So she was determined to teach us frugality
and how we should behave!

I remember the time we had churned butter
and had lots of buttermilk.
Now buttermilk is sour and really kinda stinks;
but Grandma was determined to prove to us
that it was good to drink.

I remember her sitting in the shade
in her rocking chair,
drinking buttermilk, smacking her lips
and letting on like she was the only one having fun;
but it tickled Dad and us grandkids half to death
when it gave Grandma the runs.

There was the day when Grandma came
and it was chicken butchering time;
again she wanted us to save everything,
even if it wasn't worth a dime.

She said it was most wasteful
if we threw out chicken feet.
So she set out to prove to us
that they were good to eat.

She would boil those things in a pot
and then remove the yellow skin.
She'd sit back and suck those bones
and really smack her lips,
and tell us they were good for sure.
But she wasn't about to fool this farm kid
'cause I had seen those very same chicken feet
scratch in cow manure.

I think the last time Grandma came to visit,
I was a teenager then.
She said I was wasting my life
if I wasn't working like the men.

Now we had a big front porch
and there were fly specks on the walls
and when Grandma saw such a sight
she really was appalled.

She said this will never do;
Billy, get some soap and water.
I have a job for you.

I knew I had been sentenced
and I couldn't get out of it.
I knew that I would do the work
and Grandma just would sit.

I scrubbed those walls and scrubbed some more
until my arms would ache.
I thought this crazy notion of Grandma's
would really take the cake!

So I kept on scrubbing
while Grandma sat in her rocking chair.
She had just one sole purpose,
to make sure that I stayed there!

I scrubbed until my fingers hurt
and they were getting sore,
you see those fly specks had been there a long time,
a dozen years or more.

Grandma said keep on scrubbing,
surely those fly specks will come down.
I felt just like a convict, sentenced to hard labor,
when Grandma was around!

At the time it's hard for kids to see
any good come from such episodes,
but now I know;
I was being prepared to take orders from
a foul-mouthed sergeant
when later to the army I would go.

There was the day I went hunting
and killed a jack rabbit.
I was glad that I hit one.
I took it to the house...to prove what I had done.

Then Grandma lit into me
and said I was wasteful,
and I was sinful to kill a rabbit just for fun.
She went on to brag
how she had raised two fine boys
and they never owned a gun!

It was sometime later
I thought everything was going fine,
until Grandma came out and noticed
some horseradish growing in our north fence line.

She thought this must be harvested;
she began to make a fuss.
She said we should be grateful
for what God had given us.

So to humor Grandma
and let her have her way,
we dug up those roots
but we knew that she would pay.

We washed those roots
and took them in the house.
She said it would be a terrible loss
if we didn't grind them and make horseradish sauce.

That night when we had supper,
we each had a piece of meat.
Then Grandma covered hers
with horseradish and she began to eat.

Now Grandma liked the horseradish
she'd gotten from the store.
But it was mild and watered down
and she could eat a whole lot more.

So when she took a mouthful,
little did she realize
that this was pure and this was stout
and it brought water to her eyes.

Now seeing Grandma eat hot horseradish,
that made quite a sight,
and us grandkids all kinda snickered
when Grandma drank a lot of water yet that night.

Now that I am older
and have seen a lot more of life,
I've always wondered why Grandpa
wanted Grandma for a wife.

Grandpa was like Zacchaeus,
a wee little man, he didn't stand a chance.
When it came to their family life,
Grandma definitely wore the pants!

Now Grandma was convinced
she was living according to God's Plan
because when it came to thinking,
she could out think any man!

You may think I've been rough on Grandma,
but this poem is true, I really haven't lied,
and I think some folks were kinda relieved
when they heard that Grandma died.

Now if Grandma is up in heaven,
that 's where someday I expect to be.
Surely God in his mercy
will keep her away from me.

The Bible says that in heaven
there are many mansions;
there is no night or darkness there.
There will be no need to light a torch.
But I hope when I get there,
someone will make Grandma scrub
the fly specks off the porch!

The Waiting Room

We all go to see our doctors
when we are feeling ill.
They send us to the waiting room
but the waiting room is filled.

Once I get in that room,
if I'm fortunate enough to find a chair,
I begin to look the crowd over
and wonder why each one should be there.

There are countless young mothers
each one with tiny tots,
no doubt for childhood inoculations,
or do they still just call them shots?

There are some like me of middle age
and some that are getting old.
No doubt some have influenza
and some may have the common cold.

Sometimes a grandmother comes along to help the
mother
who already is twice blessed.
And now she'll hear the news
that soon there'll be another little one
to join them in the nest.

One time I saw a young couple with five kids
between them
and another one on the way.
It may have been a vasectomy
that she had in mind for him that day.

There may be a young couple there to get a
blood test
so they can be a bride and groom.
You sure see all kinds of people
in the doctor's waiting room.

As I look the whole crowd over
and assess why they are there,
I'm sure most have health insurance,
some may pay cash and some rely on Medicare.

Then I look through the magazines and it is plain
to see
They don't treat many cowboys or cowboy
wanna-bes.
They don't have the <u>Western Horseman</u> or <u>True West</u>
with its stories about the U.S. Cavalry.

I hear them call the others' names
and down the hall I see them go.
My doctor must be gettin' older
he seems to be runnin' kinda slow.

I leaf through all the women's magazines
about how you can develop rock-hard abs,
or larger bulging pecs.
In Redbook there is an article about
how older couples can have more exciting sex.

I wait and wait and wait some more
and wonder if they'll ever get to me
before it's time to go home
and start to doin' chores.

I twist and turn and rearrange
the jacket folded in my lap.
If waiting rooms just had recliner chairs,
I could take a little nap.

At last a sweet young nurse stands in the door
and then she calls my name.
And then I seem to be all stoved up
and I walk a little lame.

I follow her down the hallway to a little bathroom
and she hands me a tiny cup.
She says "Sir, we need a specimen.
Would you kindly fill this up.

I'll be in the adjoining room
reviewing your health insurance plan."
I want to say, "Dear lady,
you kept me in the waiting room so dang long,
I could fill a three pound coffee can!"

At last the doctor sees me.
He checks my blood pressure and my pulse
and says I'm a little over weight.
He suggests that when I go to the pasture
to check the cows I should do more walking
and leave the pickup at the gate.

Now he may be an educated man
but this wouldn't work at all.
I sure don't have a hankerin' to get run over
by a smoky Simmental.

He doesn't know that I have cows
that will stomp you in the ground.
Or that I'd have to rely on a neighbor
to call the ambulance to haul me into town.

He gets me all checked over
and says I'm not suffering any serious ills.
But just to be on the safe side,
He'll write out a prescription
to get some little pills.

He asks me lots of questions like
"How much I eat?
How much I drink?"
and, "How well do I sleep?"
and, "If I'd get short of breath a climbing stairs
if they were kinda steep?"

71

Then he gets real personal
and asks if my stools are soft or hard?
but what he wants to see the most,
is my . . . health insurance card.

At last he is done with me
and says, "The insurance company will be billed.
Don't forget to stop by the pharmacy
to get the prescription filled."

They have pills to keep girls from getting pregnant
and lots more if they do.
Why, they have pills for just about
anything that could be ailin' you.

They have pills for headaches
and some to help you relax.
They have pills to keep you regular
and pills for aching backs.

They can load you up on vitamins
if vitamins are what you lack.
But it always gets to me
how they want you to make one more appointment.
They keep you coming back.

Like the time I had a hurtin' foot,
intense pain was in my toe.
It really hurt so bad I could hardly go.

The doctor took one look at me
and said, "You have the gout.
Take these pills for 30 days
and make an appointment on your way out."

Now what I think we really need
is a lot more one-shot cures.
Like when a pig gets altered
or you cut off a rooster's spurs.

Like when we are workin' calves
and run them through the chute.
They get Lepto, Red Nose, 7-Way
and a nasal in the snoot.

It doesn't take us very long,
just long enough for his fear of man to be renewed.
And when the operation's over,
he walks away with an adjusted attitude.

Now and then a doctor becomes puzzled.
He doesn't know what to do.
So he'll refer you to a specialist
to cure what's ailin' you.

Now, there is a famous doctor.
Weekly he makes the evening news
and if you should get referred to him,
I hope you will refuse.

Please, oh please, don't go see Dr. K.
He'll only make things worse.
You may fly there in a jumbo jet.
But, you'll come back in a hearse!

Farming's Changed A Lot

Farming sure has changed a lot
since you and I were boys.
The John Deere "A"s and Farmall "M"s
that used to do the heavy work
are now hardly more than toys.

Remember back when we were kids
and some tractors were still on steel,
you'd bump your shins on those steel lugs,
and it would hurt so bad you'd really want to squeal.

My Dad's first tractor that I remember
was a '38 John Deere B.
I was just a little kid
so it seemed awfully big to me.

It was for several seasons as I remember
that Dad would say,
"If we have a pretty good farming year,
we'll do away with those steel wheels
and put rubber on the rear."
That tickled us boys half to death
'cause then when we drove her down the road
we could drive her in high gear!

Dad said that "B" was so handy,
not like a steam engine
that took ten acres just to turn around.
And unlike the big old Rumley tractors,
it didn't pack the ground.

It pulled a seven foot tandem disc in second
gear a-discing down corn stalks.
You'd set her at 2/3 throttle
and listen to that little two cylinder engine talk.

I bet it was a hundred times that I heard Dad say,
"You can really get a lot of farming done
if you just keep that tractor going
and you don't have to stop and rest the horses some."

That little "B" did everything
that seems quite primitive as I think back on it now.
When Dad was preparing potato ground
it pulled a two-way one bottom plow.

It cut the stalks; it worked the ground
and it even ground the feed.
It moved the hog sheds to clean ground
when there was the need.

Then in the winter of '49
it moved all of our equipment to the new place
where Dad watched his boys grow until the day
he said we could use some more tractor power
so Dad bought a John Deere "A".

Now it was just for heavy work,
a bigger plow, a bigger disc,
but it was not for haying with.
But we did put on a two-row cultivator
because it had a power lift.

Well since those days we've seen the tractors grow
because getting bigger was the rule
and when traction and ground compaction became
a problem
someone invented duals.

We saw the one-row corn pickers come
and the two-row corn pickers go.
We've seen three-point blades and front end dozers
that come in mighty handy when it comes to moving
snow.

Yes everything got bigger
with machines that make a lot of noise.
Yeah, farming sure has changed a lot
since you and I were boys.

We saw them put electric lights on all equipment
and then farming became non-stop.
And you and I were teenagers
when corn became a combine crop.

I remember yet how strange it seemed
the first time we had some corn combined.
When he pulled up to the wagon
and put in gear the unloading spout
and as that unloading auger turned
it was shelled corn that came out!

At first there were two-row corn heads
and then we saw them grow to three then four
and then on out to five
and then those corn heads kept on growing
just like they were alive.

Today one man with a combine
and a cornhead that takes about twelve rows
can pick and shell more corn in thirty minutes
than what we used to grow.

Time is of the essence,
that is what we all well know,
and now everyone uses a big grain cart
so the combine can be unloaded on the go.

We've seen a lot of changes in hay machinery.
It would be hard to name each one
but now we put hay in big round bales
that weigh a thousand pounds
and big squares that weigh a ton.

There are countless other changes;
I could go on and on.
But with all our labor saving devices
we still have to make an effort
to find some time just to mow the lawn.

With all these changes that we have seen,
the farmers too have changed.
It does not seem so neighborly
to help each other any more.
It seems that everyone is more intent
on helping out the machinery salesman
at the big machinery store.

One day I saw a big tractor in the field
with six driving wheels across the front
and six more across the rear.
That man was helping someone all right.
The guys that work in the farm tire shop at Firestone
or Goodyear.

Remember back when we were kids,
you just helped a neighbor out,
whether it was hauling in corn silage
or piling up baled hay.
You were glad to help your neighbor
and there was no want for pay.

He helped you and you helped him
and you would even lend him tools.
We just sort of lived by an unwritten
"Farmers' Golden Rule."

When his cows got out, you put them in
and he'd do the same for you.
It just seemed to be
the natural neighborly thing to do.

There was no need for farm liability insurance
like there is today.
For there was no thought of a lawsuit
even if your cows ate up all his hay.

There is one more thing that has become
just about as rare as homemade starch.
It's neighbors helping a neighbor move
when it comes the first of March.

Remember back when we were kids
and you heard that a neighbor would move away,
everyone came from all around
to help on moving day.

They came with tractors, trucks and pickups
and each would take a load.
And they all made quite a caravan
as they moved the neighbor down the road.

It hurt down deep to lose a neighbor
but yet, a helping hand you were glad to give
because your neighbor had found a better farm
and his family would have a nicer house in which to
live.

Today it's everyone for himself,
and he'll see what he can do.
He has a need to get bigger
so he'll try to get your land away from you.

They will come from near;
they will come from far;
they will come from all around
if you just put out a little rumor
that you might rent out your ground.

Remember back when we were kids.
Listen---Can't you just hear our dads say,
"the boys will be glad to help you after school
and all day Saturday."

This too has changed
and if you could use some help
from a neighbor boy today,
he'll want to know if your tractor has an air
conditioned cab,
a radio and just how much you'll pay.

If you come to some agreement
and suggest that when he is finished
he might clean out the hog shed ventilator fans,
he'll want to quit at 4 o'clock
because he has other plans.

And if you might suggest a job
with some hand labor that's involved,
he'll want you to supply the leather gloves.
And if it is the 1st of September,
you might as well forget it.
He'll be out shooting morning doves.

Remember back when we were kids,
the farm wives would buy the groceries
by selling eggs and cream,
but this too has changed
because all across our country
our lifestyle follows a different scheme.

They no longer are allowed to sell
garden produce or dressed chickens
or eggs so that others might also save.
Now everything has to be USDA inspected,
packaged, ready to pop in the microwave.

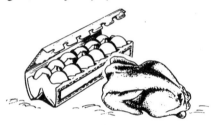

So farm wives now have jobs in town
so they can make ends meet,
to provide the kids with school clothes
and keep shoes upon their feet.

You no longer see farm wives get together
to butcher chickens by the dozen
or put up sweet corn by the tub.
But now they get together to form
and join what we call the chubby club.

If they would let me be a member
or at least plan their meeting for July,
I would come up with something different
because I am a guy.

I'd say, "Just wear a common shirt
and squeeze into your jeans.
We'll meet at my place along the south road
and then we'll walk some beans."

There they could walk and bend and stretch
and they would realize
that they had some muscles
that were not used to exercise.

We'd have our meeting last
from one till three which is the hot part of the day
and as those ladies exercised
their pounds would melt away.

The next time you drive your tractor
just take stock of all you have
at your fingertips control.
You have 3-point hitch, for power lift
and also depth control.

There's power shift and front wheel assist
for keeping you on the go.
The throttle range has a rabbit and a turtle
to indicate fast or slow.

There are hundreds of horses under the hood
just ready to work for you.
A climate controlled cab
with a wrap-around windshield
for an unobstructed view.
An easy ride seat and a tilt steering wheel
just to make easier what you do.
AM-FM radio to keep you up to date
with the weather, markets and news.

So as you ride in your sound guard cab
to muffle out the engine noise,
remember all of this was invented
just since you and I were boys!

The Cowman

I went out to chore one morning;
it was February 3.
The ground hog had seen his shadow
six more weeks of winter there would be.

Six more weeks of winter
or six weeks until it's spring.
Either way you say it, it means the same
but one has a little different ring.

One has the sound of anticipation,
the other of despair;
but winter was nothing but stark reality
as I breathed in that cold and bitter air.

My boots made a high pitched, crunchy,
squeaking sound
as I walked across the snow
and as I looked at the thermometer
it stood at 22 below.

There was no wind, the air was still;
just as still as death.
And it looked like my horses had all taken up smoking,
you could see their each and every breath.

I grabbed my pitchfork and headed for the ground hay pile;
the cows were needing feed.
Then I realized my fork handle
was suffering from hypothermia;
its temperature must have been a negative 93.

While I was there a-feeding cows in weather
where one could quickly freeze,
I wondered why I do it;
I even questioned my own mentality.

And then I remembered that all across our country
there are cowmen just like me,
out there a-feeding cows
when the temperature is close to a minus 23.

I thought of how many are dependent on the cowman
and how little they would have
if it wasn't for the cowman feeding cows
and watching them closely when they calve.

Like the feed lot operator,
with pens and pens of steers.
Or the sale barn operator, and sale barn auctioneers.

How about the boys that drive the 18 wheeler
cattle hauling pots.
Or the veterinarians and their assistants,
who make a good portion of their living
by giving cattle shots.

What about all the people that work at IBP,
they would have no work to do
without cowmen like you and me.

Think of all of the equipment that has been invented
for working cattle.
Like crowding alleys, squeeze chutes,
portable panels that make up porta-pens.
They all have little value to anyone
unless he is one of us cattle men.

You may be a professor
in a classroom of some university;
or a surgeon in some operating room performing surgery,
or maybe a big stout husky guy
who plays football for the NFL.
Or a preacher in a pulpit
warning of the perils
of spending eternity in hell.

You may be a salesman
who drives your car on down the road,
or you may be a biologist
who studies the lifestyle of some South American toad.

A bus driver, a mechanic or a pilot
making transcontinental flights,
or a singer or an actor
and have your name put up in lights.
But you're all dependent on the cowman
for that steak you ate last night.

Today we have those who disapprove
of animal agriculture,
and eating any kind of meat.
They say fill up on fruits and nuts and berries
and your diet will be complete.

Yet when they want to serve something special
or celebrate some outstanding feat,
they don't say come over for some cabbage
and some carrots
or a bowl of cereal flakes.

They say we'll fire up the grill
and we'll grill up some steaks.
This just seems to be fulfilling
a supernatural plan
that man should first go out and feed the cows
and then the cow should feed the man.

Remember the story in the Bible
of the cowman who had a prodigal son
and how the kid wanted to quit the home ranch
and go live a life of fun?

One day he said to his father
I'm tired of tending cows
and feeding them this hay.
I want to go enjoy my life
and do it some other way.

I want my share of the inheritance
and I want it now.
We could have a herd reduction sale
and sell off a portion of the cows.

With his pockets full of money
he set out for the brighter lights of town
the Bible says he was given to much loose living.
I suppose he caroused around.

He may have been attracted to wayward women
and drinking lots of wine.
He thought this sure beats pushin' cows around.
This lifestyle suits me fine.

We all well know what happened;
his money came to an end.
When he had no money,
he also had no friends.

There was no one to buy him a sandwich
or even a little glass of wine.
When he came unto his senses
he was living in some guy's hog pen
and eating with the swine.

He said I have been so very foolish
against my father I have sinned.
If I could be just one of his hired hands
at least they have a bunkhouse to get in.

So looking ragged and feeling rejected
he wandered on back to his Dad.
And when the old man saw him,
he was so very glad.

The others could not fully understand
the reason for his joy.
Until he explained to them
this one that looks like a beggar
used to be my little boy.

It was true back then,
just like today,
that no matter where a child may wander
or how far away he roams,
nothing touches an old dad's heart as much
as when the kids come home.

Dad said, "Let's set aside this day
from working, have a party,
be merry and we'll laugh.
Would some of you boys go out
and kill the fatted calf."

So to celebrate the kid's homecoming
and the end to the old man's grief,
they had this great big banquet
and they were eating beef.

Now the moral to this Bible story
has nothing to do with eating meat,
but it points to God's unending love
and how his forgiveness is complete.

When we find that we have wandered
and we have gone astray,
just come to our Heavenly Father;
ask his forgiveness.
He'll hear us when we pray.

And when we see the cross
or hear someone sing Amazing Grace,
remember it was you and I
who deserved to die
but Jesus took our place.